ALL RIGHTS RE material protected under international and federal copyright laws and treaties. Any unauthorized reprint or use of this material is prohibited. No part of this book may be reproduced or transmitted in any form or by any means electronic or mechanical, including photocopying, recording or by any information storage and retrieval system without express, permission from the author/publisher.

Disclaimer

This book was written by the author in order to free her from the pain she experienced growing up as a child. Names, places and actual situations have been slightly altered to protect those involved.

ISBN:978-0-557-96075-0

© Mae Claire 2010

Dear June,
Thank you for standing up and supporting me. Enjoy this book!
Mae Claire

JOGGING TO HELL
Mae Claire

Preface

Miracles happen; they happen every day. One does not need to be a heroic fighter or famous celebrity to have something miraculous happen to them, they must simply believe. Miracles come in all shapes and sizes; for some they are but an experience, a moment in time, and for others a miracle encompasses their entire life. I have had the extreme pleasure of sharing in the life of a friend and I consider her experiences to be miraculous. Mae Claire, the author of *A Failed Adoption: Who is Your Larimar*, shares in this book, how she has overcome many challenges to be where she is today. She is a unique person and is a person who has given great insight into my life as well as the lives of others.

As Mae Claire draws her audience in with such infectious writing, they are given a glimpse of one specific moment in time. The story she shares is truly one of courage and amazing faith. Listen to what Mae Claire has written, pay attention to the lessons of life, and know that miracles do come true. Miracles often paint a picture of a life. The picture that is painted in this story is one of strife and courageous faith. I am grateful for the lessons her stories embody in *Jogging to Hell*, and I hope you will be too. By LKM

Chapter 1

"Shut up, Shut up!" The harsh voice muttered behind me as he pushed me further and further into the trees.

"Don't pray to God, He won't help you" another voice said as the other one shoved me down to the ground. My knees were scraped by the rocky soil. My heart was interrupted.

Chapter 2

It was around 6:30 pm and the sun had yet to set over the beautiful mountains of Crab town. Crab town was small and only had about 5500 people living in the area. The area was dry and arid. There were no traffic lights, 2 small schools and many little shops called Colmades. The colmades were made up of debris and lonely pieces of wood found on the side of the roads. The roads were dusty and rough to drive on. No one would want to bring a fancy car to Crab town because the car would surely get ruined.

Crab town was a quiet old town with friendly people. Nothing really ever happened there and crime was unheard of. No one had money to buy weapons to commit a crime. Most of the people living in Crab town survived with only a dollar a day.

The majority of the population lived in small shacks. Each family had no less than 4 children living in each home. The homes consisted of a living room the size of a porter potty, a bedroom which all six or more people slept in, an outhouse that was built some ways away from the house so as to not contaminate the area by smell, and one kitchen. The kitchens were a little larger than the living rooms. Each kitchen had a sink and a makeshift stove. You know one of those stoves that one makes while camping? Yeah, you catch my drift-it was basically a fire pit.

Poverty was everywhere. Children roamed the streets rarely covering their essential body parts. Their hair was never combed and their teeth never brushed. Who would have the money to buy toothpaste off a dollar a day? Each parent combined their money to make fourteen dollars for an entire week. The fourteen dollars could not pay for clothes for each child in the family nor was it sufficient for food. Many of the children starved because they never felt full. Their bellies could never fill up.

Although the majority of the population in Crab town was poor, my family and I were not. According to the residents, we were very well off. We really *did* have everything we wanted and needed. But sometimes what we wanted and needed was just not enough to keep my family together.

Chapter 3

Ever since I was a child, I had this deep frustration and feeling of hatred towards my mother. My mother did what she could to make me happy but for some strange reason, I was not. She bought me things, she took me places, she wanted me to be successful to some degree and she encouraged me to think for myself. She tried to embrace me.

Maybe it was the way she did all of these things that made me dislike her. Now get it right readers, I didn't hate her. I disliked her. I disliked her very much. There was something inside of me that kept me from liking her. She had a way to her that made my teeth cringe, my stomach churn and my head hurt. Yes, she did things for me but she expected things for herself. If I did not do exactly what she wanted me to do, at exactly the right moment, she was all up in my grill. She got furiously mad even to the point of saying "well, I don't really want to deal with you right now." For a young child to hear those words, hurt so much. Immediately the feelings of alienation, separation and worst of all, the feeling of not belonging came in like a wave.

    Many nights I would cry myself to sleep because I could not please her. I reached for the heavens when it came to pleasing her. I gave up my weekends to care for my handicap brother. I took time out of my day to wash dishes. I did things she wanted the other kids to do but they were smarter than I was. They just said "no" and for some strange reason, she let it go. When it came to me, however, she would tell me that I was being selfish and rude. It hurt me but I learned to ignore it.

    This story is not about my mother and how she treated me. This story is about how one night of terror led to an eternity of love, friendship and healing.

Chapter 4

It was 6:30pm and I was getting ready to go on my evening walk. Every night I walked the distance of 3.5 miles. I learned to do this as a young child. The more I went on my walks, the better I felt about myself. It was not only something that was ingrained in me as a young one, but I really did feel more energized and healthier after I went on my walk. I did not do it to be skinny. I did it to feel good. But in the back of my mind, I believe my motives may have been the first ones.

My family and I had just finished eating dinner. My siblings decided to finish up the dishes since they knew I wanted to make it down the hill and back before it got too dark.

"You going on your walk again?"

"Yeah," I said.

"When do you think you are going to get back?"

"When do I usually get back? I only have been doing this for about 3 years. Come on, you tell me. When do you think I am going to be back?"

"Hmmm....ummm like by 7:15 or so- if you leave like right now. And since you are not leaving right now, you won't be back until like 7:20 or so because it takes you like a million hours to get your shoes on. After you get your shoes on you kind of stare out into space and….."

"I get your drift—yes, I should be back around 7:20 or so," I answered mockingly.

"Will you guys take care of the dishes for me while I am out? Not just washing, but putting them away too? If I don't get out I can't get my walk in."

"Yeah, but you owe us one."

"What are you talking about I owe you one. You must be kidding me. Do you remember how many times I have done dishes for you and you have yet to pay me back? Gosh, you guys won't do anything for me without expecting something back will ya…..selfishness is all of your middle names!"

"Actually, my middle name is…"

"I know, it was a joke-haha thank you for taking care of the dishes you guys."

"Have fun on your walk," said my little sister as she took a huge bite of the chicken pot-pie meal sitting on the counter. She was supposed to be putting it away, not eating more of it.

So, after I finished up with my food, I took my dishes over to the sink, rinsed them off a bit and left them and went down to the basement where my shoes were engaged in a conversation with the rest of the families. (Sometimes I really do think my shoes can talk and that they talk to other shoes.) I mean seriously, what do shoes do for 24 hours every day, 7 days a week and 365 days a year? Do they seriously just sit there?

As I walked to the basement, a shiver ran down my back. I descended the red and orange cement and tile stairs which took me about 20 seconds. There were about 30 stairs going down and coming up, it felt as though there were 60 both ways. That feeling that ran down me made my arm pits sweat a little. I did not really know why my arm pits were sweating when I had yet to go jogging that day. But I assumed that it was because my mind was getting ready to be rejuvenated.

I was wearing short spandex that really stuck to my rear-end. I wore a sports bra along with a jogging shirt (whatever that is supposed to look like). My hair was in braids because as Haitians, our hair does not just stay calmly in one place. It has to be tied up or in braids 24/7. At 6:45pm I started my jog down the real steep windy road. At the top of the hill you could see the view. The view was beautiful and amazing. As the sun set behind me, the clouds were making funny shapes in front of me. It was truly a beautiful night. I could smell the flowers all around me and hear the birds singing their most familiar tunes.

I started off going real slow. I never liked jogging too fast because I knew that if I started off too quickly, I would get tired sooner. After about 5 minutes I decided to pick up some rocks. I picked up two rocks that weighed about 2 pounds each. The reason I jogged with rocks was because the rocks helped me build muscles in my upper arms. Building muscle was always good because I lived with a family that was constantly helping build houses for the poor. The stronger you were, the more you could help with building a house for someone in need.

I started to pick up pace as I jogged downward toward my destination (the gate).

It was nice because when you start your walk, you are going downwards. What is tough is returning because everything is pretty much uphill.

Down was difficult if you were not careful. Many times I felt my feet coming out from under me. I would slip and fall but I always got back up. I *had* to make those 3.5 miles back and forth. I couldn't stop. My body began to sweat as I approached the horse trough that was used to feed my family's 3 horses. I continued to jog as I sang the song *When the Music Fades* and *I exalt Thee* to myself. Finally, I approached the chapel on the hill. This chapel always marked my "1/3rd of the way" point. I jogged past the chapel and reached

Heartbreak Hill.

Chapter 5

Heartbreak Hill was nice too because it was very steep. I preferred to walk up the hill rather than down this particular hill. I knew the more I walked up the hill, the more anger and aggression I would get out during my ascensions. So there it was, Heartbreak Hill.

"Yes! I can't wait to go down this sucker" I would tell myself.

"Because as soon as I go down this thing, I get to come right back." As I descended the hill slowly and cautiously I began to pray. For some reason prayer was the first thing that came to my mind.

"Lord God, I pray for all of those people who wronged me. I pray for all of those people who made me feel like I was not worth anything. Bless the people I wronged and made feel worthless. Lord, please be with Ella as she has to go to school and take exams this following week." I prayed and prayed-prayer after prayer.

I reached the *Mustard Seed* house which is the house my parents rent out to a group of Catholics. Living at the Mustard Seed were 7 disabled children. Each child had some kind of a challenge. I didn't look at them any different.

"These kids have no choice but to be open with their challenges. We all have challenges but we are good at hiding them. My challenge for one is remembering things for tests" I whispered to myself as I approached the home. I loved the children and spent many hours in the home helping out with their simple everyday needs.

The *Mustard Seed* was a real small house with 2 bedrooms and a kitchen. It had a small bathroom. Previously the house was rented out to a missionary family. Now, having 7 children in the house, some work had to be done. There were bunk beds put into the bedrooms and an extension was added to the place for more space. The kids needed a place to play that was outside, but way from traffic.

That day I stopped at *Mustard Seed* to get a drink of water. They were always very kind to me and never had any problems helping me or any of my siblings out when we were hungry or thirsty. They were just great people!

"Let's see what Mustard Seed has for me to drink today" I thought to myself as I jogged to the door and knocked. Luckily they were home. Sometimes the parents who live and care for the children in the house take the children out to the movies or to the beech. But I was lucky that day. The kids were home and so were the house parents who lived there.

"Here you go. How is it up there at the big house, anything new been going on?" One of the ladies asked as she handed me the pink children's glass of water. It was hardly enough water but they didn't get much clean water anyway. So I took it with a smile on my face.

"Things are good, I am constantly at odds with my mom though, and it makes it difficult to want to live there. Plus, I don't like living so far away from civilization," I said.

"I know how you feel; it is very hard to live so far away from other people. Sometimes I get lonely," the lady said as she picked a dry scab off her head.

"Off on your walk again, huh?" the second lady asked.

"Yes I am. Thanks for the water," I replied handing back the pink kid's cup.

I exited while saying good bye and I got back on the road. I had half more of Heartbreak Hill to go and still 1/3rd of my way to go with my destination before I started back home again. Around me I could see a huge mound of dirt that was used to keep the cars in place when parked on the hill. I smelled nasty garbage rotting in an old metal garbage can. I swear it smelled like the world's waste. It was only garbage from *Mustard Seed* but it sure did smell like a combination of a lot of people's junk.

In the middle of Heartbreak hill there was a beautiful tree. This tree always seemed to me to be a mango tree but countless times I was proven wrong by my siblings and the simple fact that it never produced Mangos when it was supposed to.

"You're so dumb-it is not a mango tree," my sister would say.

"Do you see any mangos on the tree? Yeah, no-I didn't think so," my brother would pipe in.

"But the leaves looked like mango leaves," I would say humbly.

"Just open your eyes yo! This is not a mango tree."

I was wrong, I could never be right with them. They new their plants, animals and trees better than I ever would. It was ok though, my focus was not on plants and animals during those times, but my focus was on the task at hand, whatever that was at the time.

Chapter 6

I was ready now; prepared to conquer my descent into the smooth and flat grounds that met up with Heartbreak Hill.

"Hoof, I know I can do this-I'm all set to go." I had finished drinking my water and saying good bye to the people who lived at the house and I was off.

"One more time, for one more dime," was the saying I loved when taking my jog. I knew that whenever I would complete a jog, I paid myself.

Three times a week I would do this and each time, I came out on top. Healthy; mentally and physically. Walking even helped me with the relationship I had with my family. Walking made it more peaceful and made life there a bit more livable.

Down I went with what I knew was surrounding me: trees, flowers, the smell of honey, the sound of buzzing bees and the oh so quiet sound of chirping birds.

"Tweet, tweet, tweet. Their life must be so simple," I thought.

"All they have to do is trust, and God provides everything they need. Why is it then that I worry? I am so much more important to God than small birds am I not? So I will trust Him for he knows what I am all about." I said to myself as I continued my walk.

As I walked down I picked up pace-just a little. I wouldn't want to get too carried away with what I was doing. I wouldn't want to arrive at the bottom too soon only to realize my ascent to the top was a few seconds away. So I paced myself. It was the only way to go when exercising. One foot in front of the other is the way I proceeded-which was the way everyone proceeds I am hoping. It would be really funny it people were to put two feet in front of the other. That would actually make me laugh.

It took me about 1 minute (give or take a few seconds) to get to the bottom of the hill from the *Custard Beans*. And I promise, I was not jogging down it. I was slowly pacing myself so as to make sure that each step was succinct with the other. I looked behind me and there it was, the Hill- oh the marvelous hill that I would soon be going up. "Oh, I can't wait to go back up that mother," I said in a sarcastic tone.

    I broke a sweat going down the hill; I knew for sure I would break a sweat going up the hill. I couldn't help that I was Haitian-it does not matter what we do, we sweat while doing it. I threw a quick kiss to the hill to let it know that I would be back to walk on its' back again. As I began to walk again and speed up, I felt the breeze on my face. I picked up pace fast enough to where I was at a steady Jog. The breeze came in spurts now. First full blown and then ever-so-often. The breeze often took a liking to my armpits. It found favor with it and all the nasty sweat I had felt under there quickly dried up. It felt good to have dry underarms. "Are these stains gonna stick to my clothes forever? Can I get these out?" are questions I've asked myself each time I went jogging. You would think that by then, after jogging a good 500+ times, I would have the answer. But NOOOOOOOOOOOOOOOOOOOO---not me!

At this time, I was near the river. The river was always nasty. It had gross bugs in it and bovine and equine were always using it to dispose of their wastes. My mom never wanted us kids to play in there and now I understand why. As a foster mother of 1, I found myself to be very picky when it came to allowing my little girl to play in dirty water, let alone waste.

"But mom, it is just water," she would say in a frustrating voice.

I would then say "do you know what is in that water? Well, you know how people go to the bathroom in toilets? Animals go to the bathroom in rivers and on the sides of the road." She would later say "Acko" which is a Spanish term for "eww". I hope that no mother would freely allow their children to swim in such nastiness. I would then have to wonder what kind of a mother they are and why the God of the universe even permitted you to be a mama.

But now the river was cool and looked so good. I could jump right in there. I could take off my shoes and all of my clothes, lay them by a tree, and then lay flat so that the whole river would cover my body. I was so hot. It had to be about 96 degrees out even though it was evening.

"If I get into the water now, who knows who would be around."

Many times peasant kids swam in the rivers' water.

"Or they liked to watch the "rich" people's kids swim naked in the water. But I wanted to swim so badly!" I stopped to stare at the river.

I wanted to marvel in the beauty it brought me and the peace it bestowed upon me. I desired to be immersed by its beauty for it surrounded me everywhere I went. But I stopped looking out at the river after I remembered my task and my goal. It was almost dark now and I had to finish my walk so that I could be back before it got pitch black. I wanted to be back in time for our evening activities.

"Your turn, it is your turn to put down your cards Mae" one of my sisters would tell me.

"No, I am pretty sure I just went," I would

tell them as we would always play a fun game of cards.

I held my head up and continued with my jog.

I soon was to approach the gate. This gate stayed locked because we didn't want any intruders visiting. We were weary of who they were or what they would be doing there. So we kept it locked. I jogged faster and faster to touch the gate. I knew I had reached the first half of my journey when I touched the gate. And yes, I actually did go and physically touch the gate. It was a sign for me. It was a kind of symbol. As I turned around to go the way I came, I heard a voice. "Mae, que haces? Estas corriendo" the old man at the gate asked. And I would always say the same thing. "Yes", that I was jogging and that I only had a little more distance to go before I would be finished for the evening.

Chapter 7

He was our guard. He was such a nice man with such a good heart. His desire to serve people was amazing and the best thing about him was that he did not expect anything back from anyone. He was solely devoted to the family he was guarding and that was us at the time.

I took a moment out of my jog and walked over to where he was sitting. He had a cigar in his mouth and a small hand radio on his left shoulder. My parents gave him that for Christmas one year. Without that, he wouldn't have any entertainment. So he was entertained there by his lonesome. He had no one to talk to except for the girls who walked to the river every once in a while. The girls he talked to were all underage. He had no concept of morals or ethics when it came to women. He would easily ask a thirteen-year-old out, but mainly to get into her pants.

He was about 65 years old had only one person to go home to: his wife. Most of us would think that is good enough because many of us are even lonelier than he was. So whenever I took my walk to the gate and back, it was a big ordeal for him. He got excited to see me and then he wanted to talk to me for hours and hours.

He too offered me water and many times he offered me food from his little lunch pail. I would always decline because I had more than enough food and drinks up at my house and he was a very poor man. He had nothing. He took the job as a watchman during a desperate search to feed his wife and extended family.

"Why is it that poor people are so much more willing to give up what they have than rich people? It makes me sad because I want to be like them. I want to be able to give up everything I have." I thought to myself as I extended my hand to shake his.

But when you come from an affluent family, the idea of poverty is different. Thankfully, my mother did a great job at introducing me and my siblings to the poor culture.

I held my other hand out and indicated that I wanted him to give me "five" and he did. He was faithful in that sense. But then he got sad as I continued to head back to the big house. "Adios" he would say as I started my jog back towards my home. "Adios," I answered with a smile and a wave.

Chapter 8

To the left of me were hills. On the hills there were cows grazing. Whenever we would drive down this road coming from my house, my father would take a look on his right side, and just stare at the cows. "Wow, those cows sure do a good job of taking care of my grass" he would say with a smile.

"Dad, what is so interesting about the grass? It is just grass. That is all it is, grass! Who cares about grass!"

"I do," he would say.

"I love the grass. It is so beautiful and when the grass grows green, the cows can eat it. It is a cycle that goes round and round."

"Ok dad, sure." I answered ending that particular conversation.

I picked up pace once again. I jogged over the small hills, and I reached the river in no time. At the river I saw a stray dog. There are tons of stray animals where I lived. People didn't have money to feed themselves, let alone, feed dogs. So they just kind of ran around without food, water or owners.

I went to touch the dog and he growled at me.

"Well, stupid dog, I am trying to be nice to you, why are you growling at me damn it?!" I walked away from the river faster than I got to it.

"I hope that dog does not try to run after me while I am going up the hill. I don't want to get bit. All of a sudden, I see one of my family members drive down in our pick up truck. He asks me if I want a ride back up to the house.

"I really shouldn't" I said.

"If I did, then my exercise commitment would be lost." So I turned down the offer. He was heading to the gate to drop off some food for the guard I believe.

"Bye," I said waving at him.

 "I'll see you in about 20 more minutes." Little did know that those twenty minutes would result in 6-8 hours of complete terror.

Chapter 9

I started to walk up the hill but instead of walking like I normally did, I turned around and walked backwards. I wanted to work out my hamstring or thigh muscles and my calves. So I did. I walked up that hill slowly. I reached the *Mustard Seed* house for the handicap children and just waved. I continued to walk. I picked up more rocks on my way back up to emphasize my muscles.

"I'm almost there. I'm almost at the top of the hill. I can do this," I said to myself.

"There it is. The tippy top of the hill. Now, from here it is pretty much 'smooth sailin'. I'm excited. I get to go home and play some evening games before bedtime." I thought to myself.

I huffed and puffed because the workout was killing me. I knew I was going to regret my calf and hamstring workout.

"Ouch, this is going to hurt like hell tomorrow morning." I said to myself.

All of a sudden, as I reached the top I saw a man in a mask. I quickly pinched myself to see if I was dreaming…. "wake up Mae, wake up…"

Chapter 10

But I *was* awake. This was *really* happening. "I'm going to get raped." Was the first thing I thought of when the first man with the mask told me to come here. He took me behind the hill and to my amazement I saw not just one thief, but 2 more. They all had guns. All three of them. In fact, I don't even remember if there were more. All I remembered was seeing camouflage clothing, masks and guns.

"Oh Lord," I began to pray.

"I don't know what is going on or what is happening but I pray that you get me through this."

"Shut up, Shut up!" The harsh voice muttered behind me.

"Don't pray to God, he won't help you," another voice said as he pushed me down to the ground.

I knew that once the man said that, I was in trouble. These were not nice people. They had come to only do harm.

Within seconds I had a blind fold around my head covering my eyes. I couldn't see a thing. Everything around me all of a sudden went dark and I began to shake.

"Cuantas personas viven en esa cas?" the man asked me. I told him that I didn't know how many people lived in that house. Then he asked me if I lived there too.

I wasn't sure what to say. Would I be hurt if I said no and later they found out that I did, I would I be rapped? Killed? Strangled? I thought that the first thing I should do is offer another prayer up to God.

"Lord, if I die please make sure that my parents know that I love them very much. Please tell my foster daughter that she was the number one love in my life. Please Lord, let her know that I love her very much and that I will wait for her when she comes to heaven." I felt some reassurance as all of a sudden a chilly breeze blew on my face. It was a feel of "It's going to be ok".

Strangely enough I smiled in this awkward and life threatening situation. My smile spread across my face and I held my head up high. I was scared, no doubt about that. I was scared but God made me feel safe.

Once my eyes were covered up, another man took my hands and tied them behind my back with string. I believe it was string but this happened about 9 years ago and I don't quite remember exactly what it was.

The string was tight. I tried to get my hands out of it and they said

"No lo intentas." So I didn't try it. They told me if I did they would kill me right then and there. The smart thing to do in this situation was to obey.

Because my eyes were covered, I could not see anything around me. I knew that it was dark now because they had held me hostage for about 15 minutes before they captured my house guard.

My house guard was walking up the hill as he did every evening at around 8pm. It was usually a safe time to come up because it was still decent out.

As our guard came around and over the Hill two of the men attacked him as one stayed with me. They hit him with their gun and they threw rocks at his head. I felt the earth tremble as the helpless man struggled for his life. Two of the men held him down on the ground and told him to be quite and to not fight back.

"No haga nada." I told him, because if he did anything or tried to fight back they would probably kill us both.

"Esta bien," he said and humbled himself on the ground.

I turned my head upward and tilted my eye balls downward. By doing this I was able to see below my glasses. With this, I saw that the house guard was bloody. He had blood on his teeth, and his shirt had been ripped completely off his body. I don't know if the men had ripped his shirt or if he had come walking up the hill without one because of the heat of the night. But he was battered and bruised and I could see, as his lips trembled that he wanted out.

The man saw me looking and he yanked my head back downward so that I couldn't see what was going on. The yank hurt because I felt something in my neck snap. I told the man he had snapped something and he actually apologized. I asked him what it was that he wanted and the man said that it was money. It was around Christmas time and all he wanted was money so that he could buy presents for his children.

"Porque no pides" I asked him. He said that the reason he didn't ask was because he knew people wouldn't give him money. So he felt he had to rob and steal.

"Pero porque mi casa," I asked him. I should have known the answer. We were rich, that is why they chose my house.

"Pero no tenemos nada," I told the man. I told him we didn't have anything. Who was I kidding? When you looked at my home from a distance, it was clear that we had the world.

"Claro que tienes, estas rica" he said. You're rich.

"Cuantas personas?" the man asked me again. I told him that I didn't know how many people were up there at the moment.

He must have known that my family often had missionaries up to the house and they wondered if they had come at a bad time.

"It is always a bad time to rob and hold someone hostage." I said to myself as I felt tears coming to my eyes. They started coming and I couldn't stop them. And then, all of a sudden I saw one of my family members return from the gate. He had finished delivering the food to the guard at the gate. As the robbers noticed the car, they drug both me and my house guard behind the hill. They were not gentle. They were very very violent with me and the guard.

"Ay" the guard yelled. "Me duele."

Chapter 11

"It hurts it hurts" our guard kept yelling as they took his leg and drug him behind the hill.

"No importa," the man said. I don't care.

"We are not here to ensure your safety; we are here to keep you away so that we can rob that house."

My heart cried out for him.

"Oh Lord," I cried.

"Why me? Why us?"

The car came up the hill and around the corner.

"Podemos matarlo" one of the robbers said.

"Don't do that because then we won't be able to get up to that big house. We would have to take care of him here and somehow hide him. Plus, he is American. If we shoot an American, we are going to pay big time." Another guy told the first man.

The men didn't know that I was not an American. But if they had known, they would have shot me immediately. They assumed I was American because I lived in that house with all the other white Americans. But I was Haitian. And with that, they could have done anything they wanted with me. And they would have.

"God, don't let them touch me please. I can't take that again. You know my past and I don't want that to be a part of my present." I pleaded.

I heard God say "I love you". But maybe it was just me, trying to make myself feel better. Often times I hear my own voice say things like "I love you" and "things will be ok". The reason my brain does this I believe is because I read scripture and that is what God tells me in scripture. So in a way, God is speaking those words to me even if it is really me saying them.

I believe God loves me and wants the best for me.

"This is only a growing and maturing experience," I thought to myself. But I didn't think my growing experience would mean that my family members would be physically hurt, not to mention, emotionally scarred for life.

The pick-up truck drove away. Once we saw it disappear over the mini hills, both me and the guard were pulled out from behind Heartbreak Hill.

"Vamonos," one of the men said.

And so the walk started; the walk to my big house.

"MAE" I heard someone yelling.

"MAE? ARE YOU THERE?"

I knew, without a doubt that voice was my mother's. A daughter knows her mother's voice. She knew I was in trouble.

"Digale que tu estas bien" the man said to me. Tell her that you are fine.

Knowing in my heart that I was not fine, my voice trembled as I yelled back "I'm fine mom".

Don't tell her that you are held hostage the other man said. If you do, we will shoot you. Tell her that you will be there in a few minutes.

"I'm coming mom. I'm held hostage," I shouted out of anger. Would they really know that I said that? They didn't speak English. So I used that to my advantage. I shouted that to her not just once but 3 different times. I wanted her to know that I was not in a good place and that they needed to call the police.

Chapter 12

"I can't hear you….." my mom yelled back.

"What did you say? You are too far away."

"No hables mas," the robber said. Don't speak any more. If you continue to speak to her, she will know that something is wrong. At this point I was predicting what the men would say.

I started to cry because I knew that she didn't get my message. We were coming and she had no warning.

Chapter 13

But some how, as a mother, she knew the tone in my voice was off. She knew something was wrong because I didn't sound right. Something sounded off. After she said "you are too far away" she didn't ask any more questions or scream out for me any more. The man in the car that had driven up while I was held hostage let her know something was wrong as soon as he arrived to the house.

The walk continued. We were by the chapel where we had a beautiful horse grazing to my right. There were so many rocks and pebbles it made it hard for me to walk. It made it especially hard because I could not see. My eyes were still covered with the handkerchief and my hands were still very much tied.

"Lord, how am I going to get out of this one? Why me?" I prayed once again.

"What have I done wrong to you Lord? I know that I had many bad thoughts but none of them really came to fruition. Are you punishing me for not coming to you sooner? Am I no longer your child?" I wondered as the walk grew increasingly more burdensome.

Chapter 14

"I love you" is all I heard from a voice inside my head. But there was never an explanation to my situation. Sometimes I wondered why he never takes the time to explain certain situations that happen to people. Like why there is world hunger, poverty, child prostitution, adult forced labor, child labor, molestation and abuse, angry parents, hurting parents and much more.

"I love you" is what I continued to hear over and over again.

"I'll take what I can get" I thought as I tried to squeeze out a smile.

The sun was down now and it was pretty dark out. I had surpassed the 7:20 mark that I had discussed with my siblings. I know they were beginning to get suspicious because they knew that I could make the entire jog in less than my allotted time but I was giving extra time in case I wanted to look at the grass like my dad did.

"Fat chance I'll be doing that" I thought to myself.

"I wonder what they were thinking, I told them I would be back by 7:20". I thought.

"Que hora es?" I asked the man walking to my right.

"Como que que hora es?" he growled at me.

"El tiempo…la hora…que hora es" I repeated.

"No me preguntes de la hora muchacha-para que quieres saber de la hora?"

"Por que quiero saber," I said. I just want to know what time it was. Was that too much to ask?

The man looked down at his watch. He so happened to have a watch with him and I wondered if he had stolen the watch from a previous hostage situation. The watch was probably really fancy with gold and silver mixed inside of it. It was probably the nicest watch I had ever seen in my life. But of course there was no way of finding out any time soon because I was blindfolded.

"Son las 7:40," he said.

"Damn, I am 20 minutes late according to my chat with my siblings. I wonder what they are thinking. Or, do they even care?" I whispered to myself.

"Como llegamos a la casa?" the man asked.

"Sigue derecho el camino y deberemos llegar en menos de 15 minutos. Pero yo no puedo ver nada. Si quires que te ayude, vas a tener que quitarme mi bandana." I explained to the man after he asked how to get to my house. I told him that if he wanted me to guide them to my house, they would have to remove the bandana from my eyes so that I could see. I knew that if I had the bandana off, I would have better bearing and I would later be able to identify them in a police report.

"Esta bien," the man said surprisingly. He took the bandana off of my eyes. He was obviously not a professional in my opinion because a true professional would not allow the victim to see them in full.

So the bandana was off and I was able to see a lot better. I looked behind me to see where I was for a few minutes. I was behind the hill, Heartbreak Hill. I never thought I would be that close to Heartbreak Hill. I met it face to face. I had become one with the

Hill and it was not a very pretty sight. We were like two pees in a pod, that hill and I.

I walked with the men. The house guard was being held by 2 men and I was being pushed by one man. He wanted me to hurry up and get to the house because it was so late. I told him that I was going as fast as I could.

As we were walking the men were talking to each other. I heard them say that they wanted to steal the guns that we had up at the house. They also said that if they didn't have any money to give them, they would kill us all.

"What a lawsuit they would have on their hands if they were to kill a bunch of white

Americans. They would not be let out of jail and they would be tortured for life. What a sad thought. And they probably would never have the opportunity to talk to God." I said to myself in a low voice.

"I would love to live longer, but if God wants me to go home, then I must go home for I am ready to meet Jesus. I want to meet Jesus soon. There is too much hurt in this world to sit around in it." I thought.

At that young age, I didn't understand the importance of me being who I was. I thought for the longest time that Christianity was the easiest thing. You just don't do things. But as I grew older and entered college I realized that it was what you do and it was all about falling that brings you closer to God.

    If you never did anything wrong; why would people need a savior. Right? Those were my thoughts on that and while being held hostage and experiencing life in the dark, I was given the opportunity to be touched by God himself. Life is not an easy train ride. There are many stops on the way and many of them are just plain ugly. This just happened to be one of my train stops and it was looking uglier and uglier. But none could beat the train stop I had when I was 10 and 11 years old.

Chapter 15

As I was walking that dirt road, I thought of the past and how far I had come as a person. I wanted to have good memories to go with me if I were to die that night. I hoped and prayed that if I were to die that night, my family would be there to join me in my ascension into heaven. They were all Christians and had done a wonderful job at showing Christ to us kids. They didn't do it the typical way. They didn't sit us down and scare us to death about hell in order to get us saved. They didn't ask us to receive Jesus when we were five because they knew that if we wanted to receive Santa Clause as our savior we would have done that too on the same day or night. They wanted a more authentic conversion; one that made us who we were as people today. One that would allow us to want more of Jesus and not less of Him. So they lived it out. They showed Christ's love by inviting people to their house. Giving poor children a home for awhile. Adopting disadvantaged children. Loving on people and sharing what they had.

    They taught us kids to love in that way. That was where our salvation was. There was a point however, for each of us, when we decided that following and loving Christ was a decision we would have to make. No where in the Bible did it say that our relationship with Christ had to be personal. He is the God of everything and everyone. He is even the God of those people who don't believe in Him; because whether they believe or not, he is still God. Them not believing did not make him any less God. Them believing does not make him any more God. He is God and that is all there is to it. But when they believe, they are able to see what and how this God of the universe works and what he looks like in their life.

My parents were God to many people in Crab town. They were the representatives of God and the way they loved on people was amazing. Unfortunately this act of love led to a lot of sexual abuse that I endured as a young child in my early double digits.

Because my parents loved on people so much, people took advantage of me and my other siblings. We had a foster brother who was about 16 years old at the time. He was living with us because his family was involved with drugs and alcohol. His mother came to my father when he was 15 years old and asked my father if he could take care of him for awhile. Well, his mother never returned to pick him up. He was young but still old enough to know that when he touched a girl, and wanted something that was physical with a girl younger than him, he knew he was doing something wrong.

Chapter 16

"Does this feel good?" he asked me one day when I was swimming in the pool. He had his hands under the pool and he was taking his finger and putting it inside of my bathing suit. He touched me a little bit. He touched me and I knew he felt immediate pleasure. He used pressure when he did this.

"Yeah, but I don't like it" I said.

"I don't want you to touch me there. That is a private place." I wined. I was only 10 years old.

"If it feels good then it is ok for me to touch you there." He said.

"Ok" I said naively. I was not sure if he was getting pleasure out of it. I was only ten years old. I didn't even know what sex was and so I thought that what he was doing was harmless in a way. Then he started digging a little deeper and it started to hurt me. I told him to stop but he continued. He told me that if I told, he would just tell my parents that I *wanted* him to touch me the way he did. He said they would believe him and not me because he knew I always got into trouble for lying to them. I didn't want to be embarrassed in that way and I didn't want them to think that I was lying either so I said I would not tell anyone.

I should have told that same day because that one molestation incident only led to many more and eventually several full blown rapes. In the end he was kicked out of my house because my parents found out that he had manipulated my little 5-year-old brother into having oral sex with him. My little brother told them one night and my parents asked if he had done anything to the rest of us. I was too ashamed and embarrassed to tell them that he had been abusing me for a couple of years so I couldn't tell them. During those two years I had wanted my dad to test me for aids because I thought that this 15-year-old could have given me aids. I had heard about it in school and wanted to know if I had aids.

The train stop that led to that was horrific and I couldn't imagine anything worse than that. But when I saw the men as I was walking up the hill, and they grabbed me and threw me to the ground the first thing that came to my mind was being raped again. This time by much older, meaner, bigger, and stronger men. I was also a full grown woman. I was so afraid that I would get pregnant.

Chapter 17

The man continued to push me as I followed the dirt road closely. I had my head down in submission to the men and also to God. I was trying to listen to what God had to say to me. Maybe he wanted to talk to me a little bit now that he had my full attention.

Isn't it funny that we call out to God when things are turning bad for us? It is as if we forget that he is good even through the bad times. We forget that God exists even when we are doing well.

"Cuantos minutos mas?" the man pushing me said.

"Como cinco." I answered. It was not long till we arrived at the house and he wanted to know how many minutes were left to get there.

"Cuanto ninos tienes y como se llaman?" I asked him.

"Yo tengo 5 ninos. 3 hembras y 2 barones. Las hembras se llaman Lucia, Perla y Rebeka. Los barones se llaman Jose y Juan." He said proudly.

"En que curso estan en la escuela?" I then asked him. I wanted to know a bit about the children and where they went to school and what grade they were in.

"Mi hembra Lucia es la mas vieja y ella esta en tercero de bachierato, ella tiene 17 anos. Perla tiene quince y ella esta en el primero de bachierato. Rebeka tiene doce anos y ella esta en septimo. Jose tiene diez anos y el esta en quinto y Juan tiene ocho anos y el esta en tercero. Todo van a la escuela publico en Susa."

"Wow, son muy intelligente los ninos tuyos? Que son las temas favoritas de cada uno de los ninos." I asked. I wanted to know what their favorite subject in school was. I knew that I had to make conversation with these people otherwise I was not going to be able to form a relationship with them. The nicer I was to them, the nicer they would be to me and my family….at least I hoped.

Chapter 18

"Todas las hembras le encantan Lenguaje y Sociales. A Juan le gusta la matematica, y a Jose le gusta los deportes. Y tu, tienes hijos? He asked. In foreign countries it is natural for a young woman to start having children at the age of 12 or 13. Since I was well over that, he assumed I had children. The only child I "had" was my foster daughter who was three or four at the time. But she didn't live with me. She lived with her biological family. I didn't feel like explaining all of that to the men so I just said "no". He then proceeded to tell me that I needed to start having children because I was very beautiful and that a man would want to have sex with me. I told him that I had a boyfriend and he said that it didn't matter. Then the other robber said, I will be your boyfriend and give you children. I told him no thanks, that I was not in love with him.

"No tienes que estar enamorada de me para tener hijos y casar" the one man said. He said that I didn't have to be in love with him in order to have kids and get married. That was precisely the order many of the people took in this country. Kids first and then marriage. Many times the children came from several different fathers and there were also many single women. I told the man that I was not interested.

"Vamos a ver" he said. We'll see.

Chapter 19

The man got closer to me and lightly touched my right arm.

"No le tocas" the robber holding me said. Don't touch her, we are not here for that. Don't be a pig. But the man wanted to touch any way. He got closer and the robber holding me pushed him away.

"No te attrebes" he said. Don't even try it. Then he told me not to worry. He would not let that man touch me. The third man was walking behind us the entire time not really saying anything.

The third man was skinnier than all of the others. Without the bandana on my eyes, I was able to get a good look at all the men that were with me. I looked over at the one that was holding me. He was a bit pudgier with a darker tone. His hair was short because I couldn't see it out of his mask. He had hair all over his arms and he was wearing long pants. The man holding the house guard was in the middle of both the other two men. He was lighter, about the color of my foster daughter-kinda like a carmel brown. He didn't have any hair on his arms and he held a real long gun. I am not sure what kind of gun it was. I don't know my guns too well. My robber was holding the same gun and the third man was guarding all of us as we walked ahead of him. He was making sure that no one was around. His gun was also the same. I am assuming that these guns were also stolen or bought at the same store.

I am not sure if any of the guns were loaded and it would have made me feel a lot safer if neither were loaded. I didn't find that out until I got up the small hill right in front of my home.

We walked on and conversed freely. I began asking the other men questions. The answer I got out of the second man was very vulgar and sexual and he kept expressing how much he wanted to fuck me. In the United States I could report that as sexual harassment. But in this country, it is another way to talk to people and it is accepted. It made me cringe and I felt like throwing up. If my robber were not with me, I have no doubt the second guard would have had sex with me by then. I could say I became attached to the one robber holding me hostage. I started to trust him. I knew that I was in his care and that he would not let anything happen to me.

We continued to walk and we were about 45 feet from my home.

"Eso es?" my hostage guy asked.

"Si, eso es." I answered. That is the house.

At the top of the little hill we ascended, we saw 3 cars parked. There was a really big house sitting and just looking beautiful. The men took their guns and they shot at the tires. I found out then and there that their guns were definitely loaded. The shells fell to the ground and I let out a yell. I hit the ground because I didn't want any of the bullets to hit my face. I didn't want to die, I had so much to live for, though I was ready. As I hit the ground I felt my knee hit a rock. It was a very sharp one and blood began to ooze out of it. It hurt really badly but nothing hurt me more than being in that God-awful situation. My robber took his hand and put it on my head. All of sudden I felt my hair being pulled. He pulled me up by my hair as I let out a scream.

Chapter 20

"Cuanto hay? Cuanto hay?" my robber asked in a harsh voice. How many are there, how many are there? It took me a few seconds to really think about how many people were in my family. I had a large family and so it was sometimes hard to remember the exact number.

"Siete" I said. There were indeed seven people up at our kitchen.

"Ocho conmigo" I said. There would be eight people including me.

"No, no hay siete personas aya" the man said in a demeaning voice. "Hay nueve personas."

The man said that there were not seven people in the Kitchen but nine people. There is no way there could have been nine people there. We didn't have guests with us that night and I could have sworn that there were only seven people there. I squinted my eyes a bit to see if I could get a better glimpse at what they were looking at. I had really bad eyesight so unless things were up close, I could not see much.

"Si tu no me dices la verdad, te voy a matar con esta pistola" the third robber said. But I was telling him the truth, and I knew that if I didn't tell them the truth, they would shoot me.

"Es verdad" I said. It is true, as far as I knew there were only seven people there right then. Eight including myself.

As I squinted my eyes, I saw them. They were beautiful. They were stretching out their arms and hovering over my house. Two of them, there were two of them there to protect me. I swear they must have been sent by the almighty God. They were dressed in white from head to toe and a special light shown on them. I couldn't explain it to these men. I saw them and so did they but for some reason, they didn't recognize that there were angels with me for such a time as this.

Chapter 21

"Angeles?" one of the robbers asked. How could there be angels here? "We are just seeing things."

"No" I said. I definitely saw angels in my midst.

Chapter 22

To think that Angeles were real and that I could actually see them was awesome. Never before had I seen an angel just hanging out with humans. I didn't expect to either. My parents had always told me about angels and how they protected us at night as we slept. When we had bad dreams, they touched us on our foreheads to calm our fears and take away our nightmares.

"Jesus, Jesus" is what I would say whenever I would have a really bad dream. Especially those dreams that dealt with horrific things like sexual abuse and murder. I would wake up in cold sweats, shaking and crying. Mom would put her hand on my forehead and tell me to say "Jesus, Jesus" so that I could fall back to sleep. It was amazing how saying that powerful name really helped me go to sleep and to sleep peacefully!

But angels right in my front yard? What a blessing! What a miracle. It was the angels that gave me the reassurance that everything was going to be ok. But just because things are going to be "ok" does not mean that people are not going to get hurt.

"Sweetie, is that you?" my mother called out.

"Mom, I'm being held hostage and I don't know what to do…"

"Oh God" she said in a whisper loud enough for me to hear. Then she was gone.

Chapter 23

"Mom? Mom!" I screamed.

"They are going to kill me." As I said this, I heard another gun shot go off. I looked in front of me as we walked past the cars and I saw my dad. He had walked up to the house to grab a glass of water. He was in a reddish towel and he had that wrapped around him. He had just gotten out of the shower when he saw me, the house guard, and 3 other men with guns. The men started to yell at him to come here. So he obediently came. I had still yet to see my mother. She had disappeared and I saw no sign of my siblings. Were they ok? Where were they? Why did my mother just leave me alone?

Why didn't my father go with them, wherever they went? What had happened to them? These and many more were questions that went through my head.

My dad walked towards the robbers and obeyed them. They told him to put his hands up. His towel was not secure so almost immediately it fell off him. He was stark naked now and the robbers took a piece of rope and tied his hands together. They took another handkerchief and put it around his eyes. My dad asked them why they were hearing and what they wanted. He also said that if any of them touched me, he would kill them. The second robber took his gun and hit my dad on the head. I saw blood gushing out of his head.

"I thought things were going to be 'ok' God. I thought everything was going to be ok" I prayed and pleaded.

I was in shock, it had yet to hit me that I was really being held hostage and that I was watching my dad be abused. It was not something I expected.

As the blood rolled down his face, I saw a tear fall from his eyes. He looked real sad. He looked hurt. He was in pain.

"Dad, are you ok?" I asked.

"Yes pumpky, I'm fine, just don't do anything to make them mad." He said.

And then all of a sudden I heard another CRACK. They had hit him again in the face. This time though, he fell to the ground.

"We don't have money" he said in pain. He was sobbing at this time.

"We are missionaries working for the poor people of this country. We don't have what you are looking for."

But that was not good enough for the robbers. They were here to steal money, jewelry, passports and whatever else they could get their hands on. They were not here to just hang out.

" No tienes dinero?" the first robber asked. "Ensename."

Show me, prove it to me that you have no money. Take me around to every room in this house. Every building on the compound and I want to see. If you skip any, I will kill you and your daughter the second robber said.

"Esta bien" my dad said. "Pero tienes que dejarme ver".
Ok, but you have to let me see first. If I can't see, I can't take you around.
The third robber went ahead and took off my dad's handkerchief. He could see now. And the blood now flowed down his face. It was nice to be able to see more than the bottom of his eyes. His face was so calm, so sweet and so kind. Rarely did things anger him and

very seldom did he cry. But today he cried, and he cried a lot. He reminded me of Jesus when He was carrying the cross. He had the crown of thorns on his head and someone else was asked to carry his cross. The look that I could imagine Jesus having would probably be the same one my father had that night. A look of "I forgive you because no one else can." It was done to him, therefore only my father could forgive those men."

"Show me where the money is" said the third man. "We do not have a lot of time so hurry up, get up."

The bump on my dad's head had begun to swell really bad now and it was oozing white and red stuff. I assumed that the red stuff was blood. It hurt him, I could tell because all of his hairs were standing on end. He was in pain and handling it very well. I wonder if he didn't want his daughter to know that he was in pain.

"Stand up now dad" I said in a very low and quiet voice.

"Do you have any energy to stand up? I asked.

"I'm trying to but I need your help" he said.

I still had rope around my hand so it was extremely hard for me to reach over and help him. But I did my best. I used what I could by turning around and pulling him up with the little strength I had. It was hard because of the angle we were in. We had to lean on each other for help and it was very difficult to do. We literally had to lean on each other to get my father to his feet.

The robbers just watched us struggle and had no interest in helping. It was funny to them and we were entertaining them.

"Que idiotas" they said-what idiots.

Chapter 24

So I helped my dad up to his feet and the men came back to us and had us continue to walk around. The first place we went to was the basement. Under our kitchen we have a beautiful basement. My little handicap brother slept down there. In the basement we had a T.V., a washer and dryer, storage closets, a small half bathroom and lots more. There were glass windows all around the room. We had couches and a few chairs; a few stools around a bar.

Many times my family and I would eat dinner downstairs to avoid the heat. It got so hot there at times that we would find ourselves cooking our meals upstairs and taking all of the food down stairs to enjoy.

The room was also used as a party room. Whenever we had friends over, we fixed up the downstairs basement for them. We had dance parties and sleepovers. A disco ball was often put up in the basement and we would all have a great time dancing.

We walked into that room with our hands tied and my dad's body mangled and torn. We went through all of my mother's stuff. She had a bunch of things in storage and the robbers pulled everything out. Again, they were in search of money. They kept a bit of the jewelry and findings my mom kept so organized in the closet storage room.

They searched endlessly and alas found nothing. They were even madder. The one holding me turned to my father, pulled his beard and said "Adonde esta el dinero?" Again my father said that there was no money. The robber took his gun and machete which he had with him also and smacked my dad a few times. The third time my father fell. He could not get up because the pain was searing. The pain was horrible and there was nothing I could do about it. I wanted to go and reach out to him but I had someone holding me. All I could do was cry both on the inside and out. After a few minutes, my dad regained strength to stand up and continued on the hunt for money.

We took a walk to my sister's room which was down the path about 1/8th of a mile. The dogs that we had with us did not serve their purpose. They were there to guard us but instead, they thought the whole thing was a game. We walked, and as we walked we crossed over the bridge that had a pool underneath it. The pool was absolutely beautiful. It was so innocent looking and it twinkled in the sun light.

"Es tu piscina?" one of the men asked me.

"No, es de mi familia." I answered.

"Te gusta nadar en la piscina?" another man asked me.

"Claro que si" I responded.

I can remember countless times when my sisters and I would go swimming. We went at night because we liked to go skinny dipping. No one was around, everyone had gone to bed and we would sneak out, go down the stairs to the pool and jump in. Our bodies were still visible because of the gorgeous moonlight which shown over us.

Above the pool was a smaller pool. My mom tends to call it the Jacuzzi but to my understanding Jucuzzies are supposed to be warm. This one was only warmed by the sunlight of the day. I loved the Jucuzzi and I was always tempted to jump off of it into the pool. That was a forbidden rule though. If we jumped, we would surely be punished. Oh so tempting though.

"Don't you just want to jump right off of here into the pool? We are not too far up you know." I would say to my sister on a regular boring day.

"Yeah, I would love to but you know we are not supposed to do it. If we do it, we will get into big trouble. Maybe even get grounded." One sister would always say in a voice that sounded frustrated.

    Grounding, that is what my parents loved to do. Whenever we would not do what they wanted us to, we would get grounded. My sister even got grounded from her own birthday once. She never got grounded for actually doing anything bad, she got grounded every once in a while for forgetting to do something like chores. But she was the good one. She rarely got into trouble with any of my parents. I on the other hand got grounded a lot because I enjoyed speaking out. I was not going to let people walk all over me.

So if we jumped, we would suffer.

At the top of the bridge (the one the robbers walked on with my dad and me) I could see the true essence of God. Right in the midst of our horrible circumstance was the blue, purified pool. There God was. I could see Him. His angels had done the right thing. They were there with my father and I. They were even there with the robbers.

    We walked over the bridge to cross to the other side. To the right was a small path that led to my bedroom that I shared with my younger sister. Straight ahead was the path to my younger sibling's room. We walked to that room. My dad gave the keys to the robbers so they could unlock the door and let us in. The beauty of the house was amazing. It looked like a small apartment. All it was missing was a kitchen. My siblings did not need a kitchen because we all ate up at the big kitchen. Walking into the room, my dad and I were thrown on the small twin sized bed. My father's hair was grabbed I believe for the 3rd time.

"No le aga dano" I said to the one grabbing his hair.

"Callate…no sabes nada". He said rudely.

Where is the money" was what they kept asking. We do not have money….we are missionaries my father answered in a quite and squeaky voice.

But the men were not happy with his response again. They lay my dad on the bed and pushed me off. One man grabbed my dad's scrotum and with a machete threatened to cut it off. My dad squirmed and I could not believe what I was seeing.

Was this robber really doing what I thought he was doing. Was he molesting my father right in front of me? He was indeed doing so.

My dad tried to squirm away but they did not let him. Then they grabbed his penis and threatened to cut that off if he did not show them where the money was. So he said that he would show them where they might have a bit of money.

"Vamonos" the men said.

So we left my siblings room and headed back down the path to where we started. We crossed over the bridge for the second time and made a right to the nearest building. It was the bathroom. Through the bathroom you could see another small room. This room was the closet where the man in the truck that drove up the hill slept. My siblings called him the "relative" but I could never come to the point of calling him that. He was not a relative to me. He was a very mean man. All 6 of us walked inside the closet. It was real large so we could all fit inside of it. My dad opened up the safe where there was really no money. There was a passport, wedding rings and some small cash but nothing like what they were looking for. They took it, they took it all! Anything they could find they took.

"Whap!"

I heard it. It was a gun at the back of my father's head. I guess we angered them some more. My dad fell and lay on the ground. Then the men just started to randomly shoot....

Chapter 25

They shot up at the ceiling. They shot down at the ground. I heard it, it was loud. I decided to duck my head on the third shot. As I put my head down, I heard a ringing in my ear….and then…

Chapter 26

Nothing…..I could not hear a thing. I tried to talk but I could not hear myself talk. I looked around for my father and I saw him lying on the ground.

"Are you ok?" I asked my dad. No answer. He didn't answer me. I was not sure if he was alive or dead. He just lay there.

What seemed like a minute passed and I saw my father move his arm. "I'm ok, I am pretending that I am dead" he whispered to me. By this time the robbers had left us in the room on our own. We were in my parent's closet. "Pretend honey, pretend" is what he kept saying. So I acted like I was dead.

About 2 minutes later, the men came back. They saw us lying on the ground and they just picked us up. They made us walk to my handicap brother's room which was also the basement. We struggled to get in there. I was thrown to the ground and so was my father. I didn't know where our guard was. He was nowhere to be found. I thought for sure he was dead. I thought they had shot him in the back of the head somewhere and left the body for us to discover later on. What it would be like to discover a dead body, and one of our own.

As we sat in the basement, I prayed to God for the 50th millionth time. For sure he would answer my prayers this time. Was I not being specific enough? Was I not being loud enough? Was he too busy for me at the moment? What about for my father? Was he too busy for him? "What the fuck Lord…..?"

Chapter 27

How long will you be away from me? How long will you be away from my father? What have we done to deserve this? As all of these thoughts contaminated my mind I only thought of one thing. That one thing was getting the hell out of there.

In the bushes, the so called "relative" lay still. He had watched all that was going on. He had seen the action, heard the gun shots and now, watched as the men tortured both my father and I. He had had enough. He took his shot gun, which he had nestled carefully in his hands and he shot it to the moon. Hopefully this would distract our abductors.

Chapter 28

BOOOOOOOOOOOOOOOOOOO

OOMMMMMMM!!!!!!!!!!!!!!!!!!!!!!!!!

Chapter 29

And that was the last shot I actually heard that night. It was so loud that even my deaf ears picked up the sound vibrations. I knew that it was a sign that things would get better. He shot the gun and it scared the shit out of the robbers. They all ran towards the noise as fast as they could. They wanted to know if someone, such as a police, had caught them. They were afraid that they may have been caught. If a man is caught robbing, holding hostage or stealing something from another person, they were sent to jail and tortured. Well, this was their lucky day. At least so they thought.

My dad heard the gun shot and said "get up".

"Get up and let's go" he motioned.

"What? What?" I asked him with the minimal hand movement I could use. I saw his mouth moving but I could not hear what he was saying too well.

"How? I can't hear you" I motioned back to my father.

I struggled so hard to figure out what he was trying to say. He finally pointed to an open window about 6 feet off of the ground. He motioned to go to the window. As I was standing by the window he held his hands out under me. I was to put my feet on his hands, bloody and torn, and I was to jump right out of the window. So I did just that. As I was lifted, I felt an angel. Along with my father's help in getting me up to the window, the handle helped me down. I fell softly on rocky soil but not enough to create a dent in my body.

"Now what" I thought. What do I do, where would I go? I was weak, half naked and tired. My hands were still tied to my back and I had a throbbing headache.

Before I could even figure out what I was supposed to do, my father came tumbling down after me. His was not a graceful fall. I guess he was a bit too heavy for those angels.

His naked body tumbled down. He motioned for me to start running. By then my hearing had gone in and out so I was hoping and praying that he would talk to me to see if I could hear anything. The gun shots had been so loud that it left me a little deaf. To this day I struggle with hearing people speak and listening to music. I have to turn the volume on extra loud.

"Go, go" he said with fury.

So we started running. Both of our hands were tied to our backs.

"Are they coming?" I continued to ask him on our way down the hill.

"No, but if they do, they will kill us" my father answered assuredly.

So we continued to run. It was around 1 in the morning now and we went by many trees. We stopped at one lemon tree that produced "limones" not "lemons". We sat under there and from that place we could see our house. It was big and all lit up.

The Joy of being away from that home was great. We were no longer subject to those men. The abuse they laid on us was ridiculous and very painful. It was scarring at that.

"Wait, what is that" my father asked me.

I looked around and saw a figure moving in the dark.

"Dad, it's them" I shrieked. Tears began to flow from my eyes. I was too young to die, too young to watch my father die and too young to be dealing with this emotional baggage. No one should have to deal with this. No one!

The figure came closer and closer but it was not holding anything in its hands. I wondered for a minute why one of our captors would not be holding a gun. I thought…"it could not be one of them"

The figure got closer and closer. It was so close that I could see more than just the silhouette; I could now see his eyes, and his mouth. He was nude except for a pair of shorts.

"Senor" the voice said.

"Ayudame".

"oh shit" my dad said. It was our guard.

Chapter 30

He was full of blood and he had open soars all over him. He was sobbing like a little baby. He could not move very well because they had beaten him so badly. A patch of hair was missing from his head.

"Help me, Help me" said the sad pathetic voice. He had no one. The robberes had separated us and left him to fend for himself. Now he was with us and was asking for our help. How could I trust him?, I thought? What if he was one of them? What if he had been one of them all along and no one knew?

"Venga" my dad said. And he put his right foot on his as a sign of protection.

"Todo va estar bien" my dad said.

The guard did not have his arms tied so he was able to assist us with getting the rope off of our hands. He broke mine and I felt a sort of freedom. After being tied for so many hours, I could finally move my hands. My dad's hands were free too. The feeling was overwhelming.

"Let's stay here, mom went to find help, I just know it" my dad said hopefully.

"Are you sure we can wait here? Will there be anymore?" I asked anxiously.

"No, the robbers now know that we are gone and that we have gone to get help. If they would do anything, they would shoot one of the dogs out of anger. But they won't come looking for us, we are too far and it would take too long" Was his response.

We waited for 20 minutes under that "mata de limon". I was so tired I wanted to just fall asleep. So I put my head on my dad's shoulder. I was shivering out of fear- maybe someone was still watching us.

"No one but God is watching us now" my father said in a sweet and quiet voice. "Only God. Go to sleep honey."

So I fell asleep for at least 15 minutes until I heard sirens. The cops were finally here. It was true, my mother did go to find help.

Chapter 31

The cops came and dad, the guard and I ran up to greet them. They were very kind and there were not just 2 of them but 10. I felt very safe having 10 cops surrounding me. They asked me many questions and I found myself struggling to answer them. I was in shock the entire time during questioning. I was shaking and tears were pouring out of my eyes like a wave from the ocean.

"What did they look like" was the first question that I was asked. I could only describe height and width; I didn't see their eyes because they were wearing masks. I could also describe their voice if asked. But unfortunately, no one asked. I was afraid. I wanted nothing to do with those God-awful men. They had hurt me and my father and that scar would be there for the rest of my life.

"Did they rape you?" was the next question that I was asked. I proudly answered "no". I had not let them put a hand on me. I don't believe they were out for that kind of pleasure. If so, they would have raped me upon my capture beside the mountain.

"Are you telling us the truth? Because if not, you could have some kind of disease and you would have to get a rape test done. Not only that, you would have to live with the guilt of being raped and not telling anyone." They said.

"Well, that is nothing knew" I said under my breath.

"No, they didn't put a hand on my private areas. I promise you!" I could have lied to them. I have lied about that before. I had been raped more than once before and no one knew about it. I was too afraid that I would be blamed for the rape. I was blamed a lot as a child so I though that no one would believe me. Maybe when my story is read, the truth will come out.

So for them to wonder if I was raped and if I was telling the truth was valid. I was all shaken up though. Never had I been abducted before. I guess you could say that God was taking care of me. Was he? Or, maybe I was just lucky.

A couple weeks later my dad and I had to go in for questioning. We also had to try and identify our abductors. I could not. I could not remember what they looked like. I remembered what they sounded like. But I could not remember exactly how they looked.

A month later my dad and I found out that the house guard was involved in the whole situation in one way. He apparently had told the robbers where to go and when to do the robbery. But different robbers came out and actually attacked him. He did not know these robbers. It was a surprise to him too.

My dad fired him the day after the abduction and gave him pension. He paid him for 6 months of work so that he could sustain his family until he found another job. But it was not a good idea to have him living up at the house especially after such a horrible incident.

I moved to my dad's house in Susa where I lived and stayed closer to my foster daughter. It was a lot more peaceful that way anyway. I did not have to worry about any abductions and I would not have to worry about an emergency escape because my dad's house was in the city and

surrounded by at least 20 dogs.

Chapter 32

Many times I look back on my unfortunate experience. I am now 37 years old. It has been 20 years since my abduction and it still affects me today. I have dreams about it. Disturbing ones. Sometimes I see things happening in my dreams that didn't happen during the incident. But then sometimes the dream is so accurate I wake up in a cold sweat. My arm pits are moist and every crevice in my body is damp. It always feels very uncomfortable.

During the day I daydream about the abduction and I can't help it. It just kind of "happens". It could have been so much worse and I thank God it wasn't. But I believe that sometimes the smallest things will affect you. If you compare what happened to me with someone else's experience, I would say there is no room for comparison and that it would be utterly wrong to compare the two. Because the two are probably pretty different. But I say that it is our experiences that make us who we are. Without our experiences we will not be the person we are today.

Me being abducted and then seeing angels is what will hold my faith and beliefs in place. It will not be my mother, or any other family member. It will be what I have experienced throughout the years.

So should I thank God for all of the experiences I have had in my life time? Should I thank God for the molestations I experienced repeatedly between the ages of 10 and 12? Should I thank God for the parents he gave me? Should I thank God for the way my mom treated me while growing up? Should I thank God for how I was treated by other people? Should I thank God for how I treated and treat others?

It says somewhere in the Bible that we are supposed to praise him. What does it mean to praise Him? Does it really mean to thank Him? I do not know the answer to that question. All I know is that because of what

I have gone through in my life time, I am who I am.

Who am I after my molestation experiences, young motherhood, abduction, and repeated verbal manipulative abuse from my mother? I am me. The one who writes to you today. I stand tall and proud. I love my family but not in the way others do. I love my daughter and I love who I am regardless of whether others like me or not.

So if I can leave you with anything; any small portion of wisdom-any bit of soup from my soul, any wise crack-I'll leave you with the idea that things don't happen randomly. It may seem that because of a series of events, things come together randomly, but the truth of the matter is-life happens because it is ordained by something more powerful than us. I don't know where this power comes from but I have been empowered to be a stronger person.

    I sit and watch the sunset and think how anyone could think that it is just a random thing. It is not! But to each their own. Life is what guides us and brings us to our next encounter-whether it is a rape, parental abuse, beautiful family, wonderful sunset. Choose the good, learn from the bad. And while you are doing all of this; love yourself, love others, and love the one who created you-whoever that may be!